VEGAS HIGHLINE

True Story of American Greed

Dallin Barnes

DB Management

DB

ESG   GSB

DB MANAGEMENT

ISBN: 979-8-9927716-5-7

First Edition, 2025

To the countless souls ensnared by the Vegas Highline scam, whose dreams were shattered by greed's cruel grip, and to those who, against all odds, rose from the darkness of betrayal to shine in the light of resilience and redemption—this story is for you.

"Greed paints a neon dream, but trust is the desert that buries it."

DALLIN BARNES

CONTENTS

PREFACE

In 2011, I was a Mormon kid from, Utah, chasing dreams bigger than the mountains around me. A UVU student with a knack for hustle, I thought I'd found the golden ticket: luxury cars, easy money, a fast track to wealth. Instead, I stumbled into a neon-lit nightmare—a car scam orchestrated by smooth-talking conmen promising riches but delivering ruin. *Vegas Highline* is my story, a raw recounting of the chaos, greed, and betrayal that nearly broke me and countless others. Based on true events, with most names changed to shield those caught in the crossfire, it's a tale of stolen cars, federal raids, and hard-won redemption. This isn't just a crime story—it's a warning: if it shines too bright, it's probably a lie. I wrote this for the victims, the survivors, and anyone tempted by the mirage of American greed.

PROLOGUE

Lorem ipsum dolor sit amet, consectetur adipiscing elit, sed do eiusmod tempor incididunt ut labore et dolore magna aliqua. Ut enim ad minim veniam, quis nostrud exercitation ullamco laboris.

INTRODUCTION: THE NEON DREAM

Las Vegas, 2011. The Strip glittered like a fever dream, promising riches to anyone dumb enough to believe the house ever loses. Slots chimed, cocktails flowed, and the air hummed with one word: *more*. That was my gospel. At 26, I was Dallin Barnes, a kid from West Jordan, Utah, chasing the American Dream with a Mormon boy's heart and a gambler's nerve. Big house, gorgeous wife, millions in the bank, and a sleek, highline car—Ferrari red, naturally. That's what I saw when I closed my eyes. Invincible? Hell, I was bulletproof.

Rewind to my roots: a churchgoing family dragging me to Sunday sermons, where I'd torment my poor teachers with pranks and restless energy. At eight, I got baptized, swearing to God I'd make Him proud. I meant it, too—still do, in my way. Mom and Dad drilled honesty and hustle into me, but sports were my real school. Baseball, football, track—I played them all, lettering in high school like a small-town star. Sweat taught me discipline, competition built my spine, and every win fed my belief: I could be legendary. Colleges sent letters, dangling full-ride scholarships. Pro ball wasn't a pipe dream; it was my plan. But at 18, I traded cleats for a missionary's tie, called to serve two years in Ecuador for the Mormon Church. Dad wasn't thrilled, but Utah kids like me, that's what we did.

Ecuador reshaped me. I left a 200-pound jock and came back in 2006 a lean 145, my head rewired. Sports faded; I craved family, legacy, *wealth*. My big brother—my hero, ten years older—showed the way. While I was preaching in Spanish, he dove into real estate, flopping at first, then banking a cool million by year two. Back in Utah, he sold me on the game. I got my real estate license, visions of mansions dancing in my head. Bad timing. The 2008 crash loomed, and by 2011, the bubble had burst. Foreclosures flooded the news, Occupy Wall Street was screaming, and my dreams of flipping houses sank like a bad bet.

Enter plan B: alarms. A slick upstart company waved a $5,000 signing bonus under my nose—door-to-door sales, sure, but the payouts were wild. Top guys, kids my age, pulled $50,000 to $150,000 in *four months*. In 2011, when half the country was scraping by, that was king money. I dove in, knocking doors, charming homeowners, stacking cash. The plan was simple: sell alarms, finish my bachelor's, then launch my empire. Life was a royal flush—I was raking it in, falling in love, riding high. Greed wasn't a sin; it was fuel.

Then came Cody Vance. A name like a snake's hiss. I didn't see him coming, didn't know some men move through the world with no soul, leaving wreckage for kicks. My train to wealth—shiny, unstoppable—hit his dynamite. And in Vegas, where every light hides a shadow, I learned the real cost of wanting it all.

CHAPTER 1:
KNOCKING ON
DREAMS

2011 was a fever pitch. Japan reeled from an 8.9 quake, tsunamis drowning dreams on CNN. Dr. Conrad Murray got slapped with a guilty verdict for Michael Jackson's death—manslaughter, not murder. Casey Anthony dodged justice, her not-guilty smirk burning up talk shows. Arnold and Maria split after 25 years, Kate and William tied the knot in a fairy-tale blur, and Harry Potter's final flick closed an era. Oh, and Anthony Weiner, some congressman, tanked his career by sending a text of his weiner. The world was a slot machine gone haywire, and I was betting big on my own jackpot.

Topeka, Kansas, was my proving ground. Picture me: polo soaked, knocking on strangers' doors, pitching alarm systems to folks who'd rather swat me like a fly. Sixty hours a week, I'd grind through that thick, Kansas heat—air so heavy it choked you. Every door was a gamble: three-year contract or a hard pass. In 2011, with foreclosures bleeding across America, a top rep could pull $100K - $250K in just four months. That was my play—stack cash, build a future. My crew kept me sane: Garret Brown, Tyler Batty, Joseph

Liddle, Jeremy Kohler, and my boy Brad Colt, who was my right-hand man. We were like brothers that summer, grinding side by side, cracking jokes and chasing commissions like Vegas high rollers.

Back in Utah, my heart stayed tethered. A blonde beauty—my girlfriend— was waiting in Provo, her pageant sash and smile pulling me through each day. I was hustling for her, for us, saving for a one-carat ring I'd slide on her finger. The plan was clean: bank $50-100 grand, finish my marketing degree at Utah Valley University, propose, and deal myself a happily-ever-after. This was our second summer apart, and it hurt. She was in a Miss Utah pageant that summer, my family in the crowd cheering her on, while I sent late-night texts from Topeka, counting the days till I'd hold her again. It took focus not to lose myself in missing her and it took strength to keep my head in the game.

Nights in Topeka were our escape. Me, Brad the boys—we'd dive into dumb fun to shake off the grind. Pool jumps, Monopoly marathons, or Garret's wild idea to blow-dart stray cats (he whiffed, don't worry). We'd blast Katy Perry's "Firework" or LMFAO's "Party Rock Anthem," scarfing pizza, laughing till our sides split. Bradwas my brother out here, closer every day. I'd met him a year back, two rookies selling alarms, dreaming bigger than our paychecks. He was in Kansas with his girlfriend, Ashley both of them loud, in love, and bickering like sitcom stars. Brad and Ashley were my anchor—late-night talks, movie binges, the works. That bond, tight as it was, was about to drag me somewhere dark.

Summer burned out, and I rolled back to Provo—"Happy Valley" as we called it, because the Mormon housewives were popping anxiety medication like candy. Brigham Young University loomed nearby, but six miles west I was grinding at Utah Valley because my ACT scores weren't good enough to get me enrolled into BYU. I was one semester from my degree. October 2011 hit like a cool snap, leaves exploding red and gold, air sharp with promise. Foster the People's "Pumped Up KIcks" drifted from dorm windows, Occupy Wall Street's protests crackled on TV, and I was laser-focused: nail my property management internship, pass my capstone, pop the question. Picturing her gasp when I'd drop to one knee. Life was a full house, aces high, the finish line in sight.

Then, one night in my dad's damp basement, my phone lit up. Brad buzzing like he'd hit a slot jackpot. "Dallin, this is it," he said, voice electric. That call was a spark on gasoline. Brad wasn't just my friend—he was the door to Cody Vance, a Vegas party king with gold chains and a grin sharp enough to cut glass. Greed was Cody's religion, and something called Vegas Highline was his altar. I didn't know it yet, but my neon dreams were about to crash into his shadow.

CHAPTER 2: SIN CITY'S TEETH

L as Vegas, 2011, wasn't just a city—it was a lie. Built on the bones of losers, its neon pulse screamed more while slot machines ate dreams. Day or night, the Strip burned bright, faking daylight to keep you spinning. Greed was its heartbeat, luring suckers with promises of jackpots and jollies. Want a hit, a high, a body? Vegas delivered, no questions asked. But step into its shadows, and you'd find vampires—real ones, not the sparkly kind. They'd charm you, drain you, leave you broke or worse. Sin City didn't play; it preyed.

I used to see Vegas as a lark. A weekend jaunt with buddies, tossing chips at roulette, chasing laughs over blackjack. Harmless, right? Then I went through hell. Now I clock the demons on every corner. That kid slinging dice on the street? Dealer. The flirty girl at the slots, all giggles and gloss? Working girl. The sharp-dressed guy in the highline Porsche? Pimp, trafficker, or both. The punk with the smirk, barely 25? He's running the show. Vegas wears a mask, but I see the fangs.

Evil's got a wardrobe, and in Vegas, it dresses sharp. The worst wolves don't howl—they swagger, cloaked in Armani, driving Lambos, sipping Cristal like it's water. They're educated, smooth, confident. They quote scripture while picking your pocket. For a kid like me, raised Mormon to love, trust, and turn the other cheek, spotting them was like catching smoke. These guys weren't just wolves; they were a pack, and two stood out: Cody Vance and Slater.

Cody and Slater were the rising stars of Vegas's underbelly, young guns barely pushing 30, ambitious enough to scare you. Cody was the frontman—gold chains glinting, fake Rolex ticking, a party king who'd chug Red Bull and vodka and call it breakfast. His grin could sell ice to penguins, but it hid a blade. Slater was the shadow—cooler, sharper, with eyes that weighed you like meat. Together, they ran a machine: prostitution rings, drug pipelines, and a slick front called Vegas Highline. They weren't the top dogs—someone bigger pulled strings—but they were learning fast, and their hustle was deadly.

Vegas Highline was their masterpiece, a car-lease outfit that screamed legit. Picture it: a showroom off the Strip, 2011's hottest rides—Ferraris, BMWs, tricked-out Escalades—gleaming under LEDs. Lady Gaga's "Born This Way" bumped soft in the background, a nod to the club scene. They'd hand keys to pimps and call girls, letting them cruise while drugs flowed east to west, hidden in tricked-out trunks. The cash? Laundered through leases, clean as a casino chip. It was brilliant, sick, and pure Vegas—greed dressed up as glamour.

The city loved them. At clubs like XS or Marquee, they were gods. They'd roll up in exotic cars—think yellow Lambo, top down—valets scrambling, girls hooking their arms. Spotlights would swing, crowds roaring like they'd seen Elvis. Their parties? Playboy Mansion-level chaos. Penthouse suites in Vegas and St. George, walls pulsing with Pitbull's "Give Me Everything." Naked girls roamed, drugs passed like candy, orgies spilling into dawn. Cody would hold court, tossing cash like confetti; Slater watched, calculating, always one step ahead.

Money poured in—too much to hide. Vegas Highline solved that, turning dirty dollars into shiny leases. It armed their crew, moved their product, and kept the IRS off their backs. They were untouchable, or so they thought. Back in Provo, I was just a kid trying to buy a ring, chasing my own score. But Brads call, that October night, was about to pull me into their orbit. Cody and Slater didn't know my name yet, but Vegas Highline was about to make sure I'd never forget theirs.

CHAPTER 3: THE CALL THAT CHANGED EVERYTHING

P rovo, October 2011, was all crisp air and big plans. Leaves blazed like a slot machine payout, and I was ready to propose and a marketing degree one semester away. Life was a straight flush—love, hustle, faith. But trouble doesn't knock in Happy Valley; it calls. And when my phone lit up in my dad's damp basement, Brad Colts's voice was the spark that lit the fuse.

Brad was my brother, not by blood but by choice. Picture a guy who's half-Jersey Shore, half-redneck, bottled at 5'8" and 212 pounds of pure muscle. Round face, small nose, thick brows, and hair so dark it swallowed light. Tanned to a crisp from mornings slathered in oil, baking under the sun, he looked like Mega Man stepped out of a Nintendo cartridge. Girls swarmed him—not for height, but for that grin, that humor, that *realness*. Brad's mouth was a machine gun, spraying whatever popped into his head, cuss words and all. People loved it. In a world of fake, he was a live wire.

Flashy? Oh, yeah. Brad rocked designer jeans—True Religion, probably—tight tees, and big-faced watches that screamed money.

His Ray-Bans perched like a crown, gold and silver chains dangling with a dog tag that caught the light. Every morning, he'd spend 15 minutes polishing his kicks till they gleamed. We were opposites, him and me. He was a Leo, all fire and motion; I was a Libra, mellow, happy to chill with a TV remote. He was liberal, I leaned conservative. But we clicked, his energy pulling me out of my shell, my calm keeping him grounded.

Brad grew up in St. George, a Mormon kid from a solid family, oldest of three. But normal didn't stick. He was hunting deer and elk by grade school, Christmas meaning a rifle and a trail. If he wasn't tracking game, he was popping rabbits or coyotes. Trouble found him early—drugs, booze, parties. Post-high school, he had a kid with a girl he loved. He didn't talk about it much when we met, selling alarms in 2010, but that kid seemed to steady him, a blessing in disguise. Still,Brad's perfect weekend was girls, liquor, and chaos, a far cry from my Provo prayers.

That night, Brad's call hit like a Vegas marquee. "Dallin, you sittin' down?" he said, voice buzzing like he'd chugged a Red Bull. "I got somethin' big." He was in St. George, fresh off a chat with Cody Vance, the Vegas party king I'd heard whispers about—gold chains, fake Rolex, the kind of guy who owned clubs like XS with a smirk. Brad was hyped, words tumbling. "Cody's got this deal, man. Vegas Highline. It's legit, and it's *huge*."

The pitch came fast, slick as a blackjack dealer. Vegas Highline was a car-lease company, Cody's brainchild, dealing in highline rides— Ferraris, BMWs, Escalades—that screamed 2011 swagger. Nicki Minaj's "Super Bass" thumped in my head, the kind of beat that'd blast in their showroom. Brad painted it: invest a chunk—say, $25K from my alarm cash—and I'd be a partner. We'd lease cars to Vegas's elite, flip profits fast, and cash checks that'd make my $50K summer look like chump change. "It's clean," Brad swore. "Cody's connected—dealers, clubs, big names. You're in, you're set for life."

I leaned back, basement shadows creeping. As a Mormon boy, raised to trust and toil, I saw dollar signs, not red flags. My girl's face flashed—her pageant smile, that ring waiting. This could be it: the score to build our future, honest money for a holy life. Cody's name carried weight—Brad's hero, a guy who rolled with Slater, his sharp-eyed shadow, running a business that glittered like the Strip. Rihanna's "We Found Love" was climbing charts, and I felt it—hope in a hopeless place. Greed wasn't my game, but ambition was, and Vegas Highline sounded like my ticket.

Brad kept talking, Cody's charm echoing through him. I didn't see the trap, didn't hear the lie in the neon. A good Mormon boy, I was blind to wolves. But that call, that pitch, had me hooked. Vegas was calling, and I was already halfway there.

CHAPTER 4: SIGNING WITH THE DEVIL

St. George, November 2011, shimmered like a mirage. Bluff Street sliced through the desert, its car lots flashing chrome under a ruthless sun, each dealership a temple to want. Valorre Auto stood proud, its glass facade reflecting red rock cliffs, promising dreams you couldn't afford. Inside, Ferraris and Lamborghinis gleamed on a polished floor, their curves screaming mine. Neon signs buzzed, and David Guetta's "Without You" pulsed low, 2011's beat for chasing more. Brad's call had sparked it—Vegas Highline, a ticket to millions. Honest money, I swore, for my girl's smile. But walking into that showroom, I didn't see the wolves circling.

Brad was at my side, my brother in Ray-Bans, 5'8" and 212 pounds of Jersey Shore-redneck fire. His tanned Mega Man face grinned, gold chains glinting, polished Nikes squeaking on tile. "This is it, Dallin," he whispered, buzzing like he'd downed three Red Bulls. His St. George roots—hunting elk, chasing trouble—made him Cody's disciple, but his heart kept me grounded. We'd sold alarms together, dreamed together, and now we stood in Valorre's glow, ready to deal.

Cody Vance strutted up, Vegas in human form. Gold chains swung, fake Rolex ticked, his grin a slot machine hitting triple sevens. At

15

24, he owned penthouses in both Vegas and in Ivins, his Red Bull-and-vodka swagger pure 2011 flash. "Dallin, Brad my guys," he purred, voice smooth as a casino chip, sharp as a blade. Beside him was **Slater** Kassab, late 20s, lean and cold, eyes like a hawk sizing prey. His tailored jacket hid a knife's edge, his silence louder than Cody's charm. They led us to a glass-walled office, where the real shark waited: **Ethan** Kassab, Slater's dad, the kingpin.

Ethan, mid-50s, was a paradox—polished suit, soulless core. His gray eyes stripped you bare, his smile a trap. He owned half the region's businesses—strip malls, diners, addiction recovery centers he bled dry, peddling drugs to the same souls he "saved." Dirty didn't cover it; Ethan was filth in Armani, a mastermind who'd sell his own son for a profit. Slater watched him like a disciple, learning the game. Ethan stood, commanding, "Welcome to Vegas Highline, gentlemen. You're about to own the Strip."

The office was packed, tension thick as desert heat. **Mitch Carver**, the finance guy, slouched in a corner, his cheap suit screaming sleaze, smirking over "creative financing" that'd haunt me later. **Vince Cole**, Valorre's owner, leaned on a desk, a shark in a polo with a grin too wide and a long white ponytail that looked like driftwood. He'd forge anything—contracts, names, souls—for a cut. **Jaxon Reed**, 24, bounced nearby, cockier than a prizefighter, his red Mercedes parked outside like a trophy. Rich from his dad's painting empire, Jaxon's ADHD fueled his loud mouth, his all-state basketball fame feeding his strut. His wife, **Lila**, a stunning brunette, clung to his arm, her smile nervous but loyal, their kid **Grayson** at home their anchor. Jaxon sold alarms with us, ran with Cody, but didn't see the hook. **Greg Nolan**, 40s, red hair and real estate cash, nodded along, his insurance side-hustle blinding him to the con. He thought he was the smartest guy here. Greg thought he was in on the game, but would eventually find out he was being played like everyone else.

Cody kicked it off, all showman. "Vegas craves highline rides—Bugattis, Maseratis, Escalades," he said, gesturing to a BMW 750 outside, its rims catching light. "Our clients—people with money who want to lease high-end cars, not own them. You buy six, maybe twelve cars, we lease 'em. You bank $1500-$2500 per car, monthly." Ethan cut in, voice like steel. "Twenty-four investors are in, raking it. GPS tracks every car, insurance covers all—renters pay. You drop $25K each, we handle loans. Done." Brad leaned in, "No-brainer!" Jaxon laughed, "I'm getting twelve—gonna crush this!" Greg scribbled notes, muttering about "returns." Lila squeezed Jaxon's hand, unsure. I saw my girl's face, that ring, and nodded.

Mitch slid contracts across the desk, fluorescent markers screaming *sign here.* "Quick now," he barked, "bank's waiting." Six packets for me: Dodge Challenger SRT8, black with a Hemi; SS Camaro, $10K rims; Range Rover, pimped out; Mercedes CL550; two BMWs, 750 and 550. No time to read—Ethan's stare, Cody's grin, Vince's pacing pushed us. Brad signed fast, his white Lamborghini and Bentley dreams sealed. Jaxon scrawled for twelve, Lila whispering, "Are you sure?" Greg and I followed, pen shaking. Ethan collected $25K checks—mine from alarm cash, Brad's too, Jaxon's from daddy, Greg's from rentals. "Welcome to the big leagues," Cody said, pocketing the haul.

The scam was a beast. Mitch's "creative financing" meant loan fraud, Vince forged names, Ethan's "clients" were ghosts—drug runners, not moguls. Those 192 cars—Ferraris, Porsches, Bugattis—fed his empire, laundering cash, moving product. Jaxon thought he was Cody's bro, not bait. Greg missed the lie, Lila sensed it but stayed quiet, Brad was too hyped to see. Me? A Mormon boy, raised to trust, I saw neon, not knives. Driving home, LMFAO's "Sexy and I Know It" blaring, I felt like a king. Vegas Highline was my throne—or so I thought. Ethan Kassab, with Slater's cold eyes behind him, had just rolled the dice. And we were the marks.

CHAPTER 5: NO MONEY, BIG PROBLEMS

P rovo, January 2012, was a cold slap. Ice crusted the streets,
dorm windows fogged, and Adele's "Someone Like You" wailed
from radios, 2011's ghost lingering like my regrets. I just bet $25K
and six highline cars—Dodge Challenger, Mercedes CL550, the
works—on Vegas Highline's neon lies. Two months since I signed
in St. George, I was owed thousands, my "elite renters" supposedly
leasing my highline cars were people with money. Back then, I'd
seen my girl's pageant smile, that ring waiting, a holy hustle. Now,
logging into my bank account from my creaky laptop, I saw zip. No
deposit. Just a balance mocking me, and $480,000 in car loans—my
name, my noose—choking tight.

I grabbed my phone, hands shaky, and dialed Brad Colt, my brother
in this mess. His Jersey Shore-redneck voice, usually all fire,
sounded flat. "Yo, Dallin, you get paid?" he asked. I heard him tap
keys, checking his account. "Nothin'," he growled. "Not a damn
cent." His six cars—Lamborghini, Bentley, Range Rover—carried
$600K in loans, same as me, same as nothing. "This ain't right," I
said, gut twisting. Brad, 5'8" and 212 pounds of tanned muscle,

cursed loud enough to wake St. George. We called **Jaxon Reed**, the cocky rich kid with twelve cars, his $800K debt heavier than his red Mercedes. "Zero," Jaxon snapped, his basketball-star ego bruised. "What the hell's going on?"

Month one, December, I'd called **Cody Vance**, Highline's gold-chain showman, after no deposits hit. Brad patched him in, both of us hot. Cody's voice, slick as a Vegas dealer, oozed calm. "Boys, chill," he said, 24 and cocky, Ethan Kassab's frontman. "First month's always slow—renters botch paperwork, accounts lag. Month two, you're golden, like clockwork." His Red Bull-and-vodka charm worked. I'd pictured my Provo plans—degree, ring, future— and bought it. Brad nodded along, his Ray-Bans probably fogging with trust. "Gotta be patient, Dallin," I told myself, Mormon faith drowning in doubt. Cody was a pro, right? Wrong.

Now, January, I refreshed my bank page, screen glaring. Still nothing. Not a dime for two months, and I'd paid $6,000 out of pocket for loan installments, my alarm cash bleeding. Panic clawed my chest. Half a million bucks—my liability, my cars—gone, who-knows-where. Was I scammed? The word burned, impossible. I called Brad again. "Check again, man," I begged. His voice cracked. "Empty, Dal. I'm out $8K on payments, too. Screwed." His confusion fed mine, a spiral of dread. Why us? Why now? Jaxon's call echoed it—no money, just debt. Twenty-four buyers, ~192 cars, millions in loans, all dry.

I dialed Cody, fingers slamming keys. No answer. Voicemail. "Cody, this is Dallin," I spat, Provo calm gone. "No payments, two months! I'm out $25K and half a mil in loans. Call me, or I'm done!"Brad tried, same silence. We texted—me, polite rage; Brad, a cuss-fest. Nothing. **Slater** Kassab, Ethan's cold-eyed son, was a ghost, too. **Ethan** Kassab, the Armani-clad kingpin, his drug-and-rehab empire untouchable, didn't pick up. They'd vanished, their Vegas warehouse a memory—Ferraris gleaming, lies shining brighter. My cars, Brad's, Jaxon's—Bugattis, Maseratis—were air, maybe circling Fremont Street with Ethan's dealers, not moguls.

Day after day, I called, texted, prayed. Cody's number rang dead by week's end. Brad's "what now?" texts piled up, his St. George bravado crumbling. Jaxon, usually louder than a club DJ, went quiet, his wife Lila's worry leaking through his calls. **Greg Nolan**, the red haired "smart" guy, left voicemails nobody answered. I stared at my laptop, Provo's snow piling outside, and saw my life unspool— $480,000 owed, no cars, no cash, my girl's ring a pipe dream. Ethan's grip, Slater's stare, Cody's grin—they owned us. No GPS, no insurance, no "clients." Just debt, heavy as Zion's cliffs.

I don't lose. Not like this. Raised Mormon, I'd hustled alarms, saved for love, trusted friends. Now, a punk like Cody, 24, and a devil like Ethan, 50s, thought they'd played me? Hell no. Anger burned hotter than fear. I paced my dad's basement, scheming. Find the cars? Confront Cody? Drag Ethan's rehab scam public? I'd win, or take them down with me. Brad was in, his voice steel: "They don't get to ghost us." Jaxon's "nobody screws me" text buzzed. Greed had lured us—mine, theirs, Vegas's—but fight was my new god. Highline wasn't a deal anymore; it was war, and I'd light the fuse.

CHAPTER 6:
DESPERATION & GUNS

P rovo, mid February 2012, was a frozen cage. Snow choked the streets, dorm lights flickered, and Gotye's "Somebody That I Used to Know" droned from car radios, 2012's lament for trust gone sour. I was drowning $480,000 of car loans—six highline beasts, Dodge Challenger to Mercedes CL550, all vanished with Vegas Highline's lies. Two months, no payments, no word from Cody Vance or Slater Kassab their phones dead as my bank account. My $25K down payment was dust, my girl's ring a fading dream, my Provo future buried under debt. I'd trusted, prayed, waited. No more. Greed had screwed me—mine, theirs, Vegas's—but I don't lose. Not to punks like Cody, or devils like Ethan Kassab. It was time to move.

I made my way down to St. George and stormed into their police station, breath steaming, my Mormon manners gone. "My cars—six, worth half a mil—stolen," I told the desk cop, a grizzled guy with a coffee stain on his tie. I laid it out: Vegas Highline, $25K down, no renters, no trace. "Cody Vance runs it," I said, voice hard. "He's got 'em." The cop scribbled, skeptical, and said he'd call Vegas PD. I left, heart pounding, picturing my Challenger tracked, Cody cuffed. Stupid me. Two days later, I was back, summoned. The cop wasn't alone—a sergeant, badge gleaming, glared like I'd spit in his hymnbook. "Vance sent contracts," the sergeant snapped, tossing papers from Chapter 4's Valorre Auto deal. My signature glowed, fluorescent-marked, binding me. "You signed, Barnes. No theft here. File a false report again, you're in cuffs."

I stood, gutted, their scolding a whip. Cody'd played me, his gold-chain grin hiding a blade. The contracts—rushed in St. George, **Mitch Carver**'s "creative financing," **Vince Cole**'s forgeries—were ironclad, Ethan Kassab's trap. Outside, St. Georges' mellow winter sun pierced my face, my $480,000 debt a chain. Arrest? Me, a Mormon kid raised on trust and tithing? Hell no. If the law wouldn't help, I'd take it back—cars, pride, all of it. Overwhelmed, pissed, I drove to a nearby gun shop, its sign buzzing like Vegas's lies. Inside, Glocks and rifles gleamed, a far cry from my dad's basement. "First timer?" the clerk asked, smirking. I nodded, picking a 9mm Glock 17, its weight cold, thrilling. $600, paid from dwindling alarm cash. I wasn't a hunter like Brad, but I'd learn fast.

Brad was first to call. "Police screwed us," I said, voice steel. His Jersey Shore-redneck growl matched mine—$600K in loans, his Lamborghini and Bentley ghosts. "I'm in, Dal," he said, ready to brawl. I hit up **Jaxon Reed** next, the 24-year-old rich kid with $800K in debt, his red Mercedes no shield. "Cody thinks I'm his bro? I'll ram his fake Rolex down his throat," Jaxon spat, his basketball-star ego lit. His wife, **Lila**, wasn't on the call, but I bet her worry fueled him. **Greg Nolan**, took convincing. "We're out millions, Barnes," he grumbled, his more than $800K in loans stinging. "Vegas PD's useless. What's the play?" I laid it out: find the cars, take 'em back, legal or not. Greg paused, then growled, "I'm in."

We made a plan to meet at Brad's St. George apartment, the day was as peaceful as Sand Hallows calm waters, a diner lamp casting shadows inside. My Glock sat heavy in my jacket, Brad's hunting rifle leaned nearby, Jaxon's bravado louder than Brad's voice. Greg, brought maps and bank notices—loan demands piling up. "Ethan's the head," I said, picturing the kingpin's Armani smirk, his drug-and-rehab empire laughing at us. Cody and Slater, his cold-eyed son, were pawns, but they'd bleed first. "Cars are in Vegas," Brad said, slamming a fist. "Warehouses, chop shops, or Ethan's dealers." Jaxon grinned, wild. "I say we roll up to Tao, drag Cody out." Greg, calmer, suggested tracking VINs through his insurance contacts. I nodded, but my Glock whispered louder—find the cars, point the barrel, take what's mine.

No winter chill could douse my fire. I'd trusted Cody's charm, Slater's silence, Ethan's lies, and lost everything—$25K, half a mil, my girl's future. Mormon or not, I was done praying. **American greed** had birthed this war—my hustle, their con, Vegas's jaws—but I'd rewrite the end. Brad's "let's burn 'em" echoed, Jaxon's "nobody screws me" rang, Greg's maps and documents spread like battle plans. My Glock felt like justice, heavy as Zion's cliffs. Highline's cage was breaking, and I'd be the one swinging.

CHAPTER 7: RECON AND REVELATIONS

St. George, late February 2012, was beautiful. Red rock cliffs loomed, palm trees swayed, and The Wanted's "Glad You Came" set the mood. Vegas Highline was bleeding me dry. Three months, no payments, no word from Cody Vance, Slater Kassab, or their kingpin boss, Ethan Kassab. My Glock 17, bought after I realized I was on my own, the police laughing me out of their station. This sat heavy, my faith cracking. At Brad's apartment, we'd planned war—steal back ~192 cars with Jaxon and Greg Nolan. Now, recon was my game, but every step sank me deeper into American greed's swamp—mine, Cody's, this desert's.

Jaxon and Brad, my crew, were trouble together—**Tweedledee and Tweedledum**, I called 'em, because when together they became dumb as rocks. We met at a St. George diner, Greg sipping orange juice, his red hair catching neon. Jaxon, 24, leaned back, red Mercedes parked outside, his basketball-star grin smug, and started to defend Cody. "Cody's busy, man," he said, voice dripping. "You and Brad? Pawns. He's got bigger cash than your cars. Bug him, he ghosts you, tells you to fuck off." I slammed my drink. "I'm out

$25K, half a mil in loans, bleeding money on payments. Cody's screwing us, Jaxon. What do I do?" Brad growled, "Cody's a fuckin' douche bag. Pick up the damn phone and call him again!"

Jaxon smirked, loving his perch. "Brad you're nothing to Cody. But me? His boy. He answers when I call—me and my dad's money. I'll ring him, help you out." I leaned in, eyes narrow. "Where's Cody live?" Jaxon's grin faded. "I know, but no way I'm telling you. Don't know you like that." I pressed: "Who else bought cars?" He rattled off names: "Carl Iverson, Julie Broadwell, my dad, and Heather, some rich 50-year-old Cody banged for cash. Kid'll do anything for money." My gut twisted. "How old's Cody?" Jaxon laughed. "Our age. Me, Brad Cody—high school buds. He rolled Mercedes weekly back then, a baller. Got in through the Kassab's, 'specially **Slater** Kassab"

Slater Kassab—first I'd heard his family's weight. Jaxon's voice dropped. "The Kassab's moved from the Middle East, changed their names and now they own half the West—businesses, cash. Don't fuck with 'em." Brad, Ray-Bans off, nodded grim. "Slater runs it, Cody's his dog. They own troubled youth programs, car dealerships. Word is, they launder money—drugs, maybe worse." Jaxon's eyes glinted. "Saw Slater cave a guy's face with a bat. I'm tight with him and Cody. If Cody don't fix this, I'll tell Slater." His bravado stank—Jaxon loved playing king, dangling Cody's leash. I got scraps: Cody's a pawn, Slater's the fist, **Ethan** Kassab the brain, his drug-and-escort empire untouchable. But Jaxon knew Cody's address. I'd get it.

That night,Brad craved a party—code for weed. Mormon or not, I saw a shot. "Invite Jaxon," I said, "smoke at his place. I'll snoop for Cody's address." Brad, hyped, called Jaxon, who bit—hook, line, sinker. At Jaxon's, a sleek condo, they lit up, smoke curling. I'd never smoked, never planned to— wasn't part of my code, God's eyes on me. But Jaxon's squint screamed suspicion. "You don't smoke?" he taunted. Cornered, I took a hit, my first, lungs burning, faith screaming. The room spun, everything hilarious. We laughed like idiots, me high as Zion's peaks, giggling for thirty minutes. But my mission held. When Jaxon hit the bathroom, I rifled his desk— papers, keys, junk. "C'mon, Brad, find something," I whispered, turning. Horror: Jaxon stood there, sick smile twisting. "Get out," he hissed. We bolted, my high jumbling fear, depression, paranoia into a knot.

Back at Brad's apartment, Brad unraveled. "Jaxon's dangerous," he sobbed, weed-fueled, debt breaking him. "He'll shoot this place up!" I'd never seen Brad cry, his 212-pound frame shaking. Paranoia gripped me—would Brad turn, his rifle on me? I locked myself in the guest room, Glock in hand, hearing "gun-loading" clicks all night. Dawn broke, St. George's red rocks glowing, my head clear. Brad shuffled out, shaking his head at our dumbass night. We feared Jaxon's snitch to Cody, or worse, Slater's bat. I ate cereal, TV droning, and stepped outside, the desert paradise mocking my hell.

I met **Greg** at a sandwich shop, his 6'1" frame, red hair, and jolly nerd vibe disarming. I found out he is an Ex-cop, a top Utah insurance agent, mid-40s, three kids, he insured Highline's cars, bought 12 himself. "Cody pays me monthly, six months straight," he said, sipping Coke. "Lives in the Bluffs, got a Vegas penthouse, dates a model, new Audi." I spilled my truth—no payments, three months, making the payments out-of-pocket, Cody ghosting. "Something's wrong, Greg. Watch your back." He shrugged, paid, unworried. I left with confirmed names of other victims—Carl Iverson, Julie Broadwell, and Heather—but no address. My detective game was weak, but I'd hunt Cody yet.

Weeks later, when I was back in Provo, Brad called, voice electric. Jaxon had taken him to Cody's Vegas penthouse—a $5M fortress, gated, with a fountain out front, six-car garage full of Ferraris, Lamborghinis, Porsches. "Cody's the coolest," Brad gushed, high on memory. "Cocaine, weed, booze, topless girls—like Playboy's mansion." He'd snooped, learned Cody and Kassab's empire did in fact run escorts, prostitution, drugs—VIPs at Vegas clubs, crowds cheering Cody's name. Worse: our cars—mine, Brad's, Jaxon's—carried prostitutes, pimps, drug runners across the U.S., Ethan and Slater's network. My Challenger, my $480,000, was a crime mule. Greed had lured me; now I realized how deep I was in. Cody's playboy shine, Slater's bat, Ethan's empire—it was either them or me.

CHAPTER 8: CRACKING UNDER PRESSURE

P rovo, March 2012, was thawing, but I was ice inside. Snow melted into mud, BYU and UVU campuses buzzed with pre-finals fever, and Fun.'s "We Are Young" blasted from my speakers on the daily, 2012's anthem for burning bright. I began cracking like cheap glass. My $480,000 in car loans hung over my head like a guillotine, still no payments from Cody Vance or Slater Kassab in three months. Their silence was a knife, Ethan Kassab's kingpin shadow laughing from Vegas. My Glock 17, sat heavy in my drawer. My rage, a sin my Mormon soul barely stomached. I was juggling finals, a fraying love, a financial grave, and a plan to steal back our cars. Greed had built this hell—mine, Cody's, America's—and I was one spark from exploding.

Jaxon was the first crack. He'd been all bravado in Brads apartment, vowing to gut Cody one momement and best buds with him the next. After our encounter at his place he was off— seemed too chummy with Cody's and Slater, his basketball-star grin hiding something. I caught him lying a couple times, his eyes shifty, and his stories were not adding up. Was he playing us? A wolf in sheep's clothing, cozy with Cody, selling us out to Ethan? My gut, once trusting, screamed betrayal. Brad my brother, didn't see it. "Jaxon's solid," he said, his

$600K loans fueling his own fire. But I watched Jaxon closer, my Glock whispering *watch your back.*

Emma, my girlfriend, was the deeper cut. Her pageant smile, my anchor since Topeka, faltered at my silences. She didn't know—couldn't know—about the gun, the $480,000 noose, or my vigilante plans with Brad, Jaxon, and **Greg**. "You're different, Dallin," she said over dinner, her green eyes searching. "Talk to me." I lied, mumbling about finals, my marketing degree due in April. The Glock burned in my mind, un-Mormon, a secret splitting us. At night, her texts—"You okay?"—went unanswered as I pored over loan notices, tens of thousands of dollars already paid from dwindling alarm cash. My bank account bled, my rent late, my future with Emma fading like like Marty McFly in the 1985 movie "Back to the Future."

Finals were a blur—marketing stats, late-night Red Bulls, my laptop's glow mocking me with zero Highline deposits. I aced exams, but each A felt hollow, my $480,000 debt a shadow no degree could lift. **Greg**, 40s, red hair, called with updates—his insurance contacts traced VINs to Vegas locations. "We hit 'em soon," he said. Brad, in St. George with **Ashley**, his girlfriend, prepared his hunting rifle. Jaxon's "I'm in" texts felt slick, his "Vegas hookup" boasts stinking of Cody's gold-chain lies. I trusted Brad, maybe Greg, but Jaxon? He was a coin flip, and I hated gambling.

April came, Provo blooming, cherry blossoms mocking my rot. Graduation at UVU was bittersweet—cap and gown, my marketing degree in hand, Mom's tears, Emma's proud hug. "You did it," she whispered, not knowing $480,000 and a Glock waited. I smiled, but Cody's ghost, Slater's stare, Ethan's empire loomed. The diploma was ash against my debt, my heist plans, my mistrust.

I packed my Provo life—books, clothes, Emma's photo—and moved to **St. George**, crashing with Brad and Ashley in a sun-bleached apartment down the street from the St. George Temple. Closer to Vegas, the desert air smelled of fight. Ashley, blonde and steady, cooked us tacos, her calm a balm to Brad's fire. "We'll get 'em," Brad said. Greg mailed VIN lists; Jaxon texted "leads," but I didn't reply. Emma called, voice strained. "Why St. George, Dallin?" I dodged, citing "I'm working with Brad on something to do with sales," my Glock hidden under my bed. She didn't know I was planning theft, maybe worse, to claw back our cars—192 highline cars, mine included.

My financials were a wreck—$480,000 owed, rent scraping my last $2,000. Emma's love, my degree, my faith strained under **American greed**'s weight—my hustle, Ethan's con, Jaxon's maybe-betrayal. I prayed, but God felt far, my Glock closer. Brad's "burn 'em" echoed, Greg's maps pointed to Vegas, Jaxon's grin hid fangs. St. George's sun burned hot, like my rage. Highline's war wasn't coming—it was here, and I was cracking, ready to strike.

CHAPTER 9: BACK IN THE DRIVERS SEAT

Vegas, April 2012, was a neon beast, swallowing souls under desert stars. Flo Rida's "Wild Ones" pulsed from Strip clubs, 2012's call to chaos. I recently discovered that my cars were being used as mules for Ethan Kassab's drug-and-escort empire, per Brad Colt's penthouse recon. Cody Vance's $5M Vegas fortress, topless girls, and Ferrari fleet burned in my head, fear coiling like a snake. My Glock 17, and Brad's final decision to bring his Springfield .40, and a duffel of ammo were ready, but danger screamed. Three months, no payments, tens of thousands of dollars out-of-pocket, my $25K down gone. Slater Kassab's bat, Ethan's shadow loomed, but I wasn't a pawn. American greed had lured me—mine, Cody's, Vegas's—but I'd steal back control, car by car, or die trying.

Brad was my shadow, his Springfield gleaming. We hit Vegas, St. George's red rocks behind us, aiming for our 12 cars—six each— over three weeks. First stop: Henderson, a cookie-cutter maze of stucco homes, dirt yards, palm trees swaying. A silver BMW 750Li, rims cooler than Cody's fake Rolex, sat in a driveway, chrome winking. My heart pounded—was it mine? Brad sped past, parking out of sight. "That's it," I whispered, Glock heavy. We crept up, guns tucked, ready for pimps or worse. A 6'1" African-American man strode out, eyeing us—two white boys by his ride. Panic hit. I blurted my alarm-sales pitch: "You the homeowner here?"

"Who're you?" he shot back, suspicious.

"This car's mine," I said, pointing, registration in hand. "No payments, reported stolen. Police and FBI are on **Cody**—I'm taking it before they roll in." A lie, but fear was my fuel.

"Man, serious? This my girl's car," he said, pacing. "Cody know?"

"Cody's ghosted, under investigation," I doubled down, bullshitting. "Feds are circling."

He dialed Cody, ranting: "Some dude says this car's stolen, Feds on you—what's up?" I froze, Glock in pocket, Brad's eyes wide. Three minutes later, he hung up. "Get in," he growled. My gut sank. A 6'7", 350-pound giant—gold chains, Kansas City jersey, NFL-lineman vibes—strutted out, confidence radiating. Bodyguard? Thug? I climbed into the Mercedes, hand on gun, the giant in back, driver rocketing off. Brad sprinted to our car, tailing. I thought, *This is how I die—gangstered out.*

The driver flew, Vegas blurring, my senses razor-sharp—every turn, street name burned in. We hit a beauty salon lot, cars everywhere, my murder fears easing. Inside, **Tamika**, the driver's girlfriend, was all style, no threat. "Explain," she said, calm. I spun my FBI tale, adding Cody's non-payments. She nodded, spilling: "We paid Cody $20K down, monthly, no issues. Cody's skimming, hiding from **Slater** Kassab." My jaw dropped—Cody was embezzling, screwing Ethan's empire. Tamika called Slater, saying, "Dallin's here, talking police and Cody's mess." My name, now with Slater. Shit. She hung up, sighed, and emptied the Mercedes. "Take it," she said. Keys in hand, I drove to the Stratosphere, third floor, Brad trailing, grinning.

"Thought you were dead, man!" he laughed. One down, eleven to go.

That night, sun setting behind Nevada peaks, we hit a gated complex. I bluffed the guard with my "FBI investigation" spiel, targeting a white SS Camaro—orange/black leather, custom rims, 450-horse V8, turbo roaring. The owner, spooked after we found his contact, called him, and told him the police and FBI lie, left the key on the tire, avoiding us. I slid in, engine purring like a lion, 0-60 in 4.5 seconds. "Badass," I crowed, flying to the Stratosphere, beating Brad by 20 minutes. Gasoline, smoke, booze—the lot's stench was victory over Cody.

Midnight, northwest Vegas, we found my white Range Rover. Previously, Brad and I called the car manufacturers to make copies of the keys to our cars just in case we found them. Doing this allowed us to be shadow-sneaky, use the keys, and drive off clean. Three cars in one night—hope, lost for months, surged. We crashed at the Stratosphere, high on wins, planning more.

CHAPTER 10: PUSHING BACK

Las Vegas, was a predator's playground, its neon claws ripping through the dawn. David Guetta's Titanium pulsed from my rediscovered SS Camaro. It was 2012's anthem for unbreakable fools. I was simply a Mormon kid riding high in a cheap motel, sheets smelling of smoke and regret. Yesterday's haul—my silver BMW 750Li, SS Camaro, and Range Rover—had us grinning, 9 of our 12 Vegas Highline cars still out there, millions in loans choking us. My Glock 17, Brad's Springfield .40, sat ready, but our phones lit up like slot machines—Cody Vance's texts, venom dripping: "You're dead, Barnes." "Slater's coming." Fear spiked, my Mormon soul trembling. Then, yesterday's call replayed, Cody's voice a blade: "What the fuck, Brad You know who you're screwing?" Brad's growl echoed: "Pay us, or we take 'em all!" Cody, burned by Slater Kassab's heat for his embezzling, pushed back: "Cross me, you'll beg for mercy." American greed—mine, Cody's, Ethan Kassab's—had us cornered, but I'd steal my life back, one ride at a time.

Brad chugged a Red Bull for breakfast, his Springfield gleaming. "Cody's scared," he spat, Ray-Bans on. "Let's hit more." Day two, Vegas's sun searing, we hunted. First target: Brad's white Lamborghini, parked in a Summerlin strip mall, guarded by a twitchy dealer in a tracksuit. We tailed him from a dive bar, his baggie-dropping hustle screaming Ethan's network. Brad, bold as hell, strolled up, Springfield hidden, and spun a lie: "Repo man, pal. This Lambo's flagged—FBI's sniffing Cody." The dealer, eyes darting, scoffed, "Bullshit." I flashed my registration, channeling Chapter 9's bluff: "Hand it over, or Feds raid you." He froze, then bolted, leaving keys in the ignition. Brad peeled out, Lambo roaring, middle finger to Cody's threats.

Next: Brad's blue Bugatti, a sleek missile in a parking lot of a Vegas high rise complex, tires gleaming under flickering fluorescents. We scoped it out at dusk, I grabbed the key fob from our pile and handed it to Brad. "You know what to do", I muttered. Brad wandered in and caught a door as someone was walking out. Not too long after, I see his cheesy shit eating grin as he's pulling out with his Bugatti purring to life. We tore out of there, high rise fading in the dust, Cody's texts—*"You're fucked"*—burning my phone.

My dark black SRT8 Dodge Challenger was last that night, parked at the Strip club that we were tipped off to, neon strippers flashing nearby. A pimp, gold-toothed and cocky, leaned on it, arm around a girl. My heart raced—$80K of my $480K debt, my pride. I marched up, sales pitch ready, but flubbed: "You, uh, renting this?" The pimp sneered, "Who's asking?" Brad, behind me, flashed me his Springfield's grip. I recovered: "It's mine, reported stolen. Cody's under FBI heat—give it, or you're in cuffs." The girl gasped, seemingly annoyed tugging him. "Told you, Ray, Cody's bad news!" With little resistance he cursed, tossing keys to dodge trouble, pun intended. I slid in, V8 growling, gripping the steering wheel with the exhaust roaring like a lion. "See ya, Ray," I said to myself as I grinned, peeling off, Brad laughing in our tail car. Six down, six to go.

Cody's threats didn't stop. A new text: *"Slater's got your names. Sleep light."* His call echoed, fear lacing his rage, Slater's shadow—Ethan's fist—closing. Brad's "Pay us!" defiance held, but my Vegas haze was about to grow darker. Little did we know our supposed lie we were telling to these strippers, pimps, prostitutes and dealers wasn't actually a lie. Later we would find out **Jaxon** was cheating on his wife by banging **Julie Broadwell** and she tipped off the Feds to what was happening with Vegas Highline. So with the Feds' invisible net tightened, unknown to us, we pushed back, fighting against greed, hustle, Cody's scam, Ethan's jaws, this war. Six cars back, six left, Slater's heat rising. I gripped my Glock, adrenaline my new god, ready to push harder.

CHAPTER 11: CELEBRATING SOME SUCCESS

L as Vegas nights reminded me of the sirens in Homer's poem "The Odyssey", except these were neon sirens, their lights hypnotizing you with their song. Mixed versions of Calvin Harris's Feel So Close throbbed from Strip clubs, 2012's pulse for reckless hearts. I was waking in the Stratosphere motel, stale beer and regret in the air. Six cars—my BMW, Range Rover, Camaro, Challenger, and Brad's, Lamborghini, Bugatti—sat safe, half our 12 Vegas Highline rides reclaimed, our loans still strangling us. Cody Vance's texts from day two—"You're dead, Barnes"—faded as he began to cave, seemingly starting to cooperate by promising cars to dodge Slater Kassab's bat. We must have stirred some shit in their inner circles or why else would Cody change his tune so quickly. Vegas's claws beckoned. Its sirens had me hooked, and tonight, day nine, I'd chase thrills, not cars, my Mormon soul be damned.

Brad, tanned and full of chaos, grinned like a kid with a stolen cookie. "We're kings, man," he said, Ray-Bans glinting. Six cars down, six to go, we hit Fashion Show Mall, dropping $2,000 on

Armani suits, silk ties, leather belts, and polished loafers. "Million bucks, baby," Brad crowed, modeling shades. Back at the motel, I crashed on the lumpy bed, suit hung, craving calm. Brad mumbled, "Gonna walk the hotel," his code for trouble. His demons—heroin, oxycodone, cocaine, Adderall, weed—never slept. Marijuana? Fine. Coke? I'd shield him, but his grin said he was hunting.

An hour later, Brad burst in, eyes wild, a crusty smirk screaming success. "We're having fun tonight, yeah buddy!" he roared, tossing two Skyy Vodka bottles on the bed.

"Oh yeah?" I teased, old Dallin's Mormon code fading. "What's the play?"

"Treats," Brad said, pulling a foil ball from his pocket, grin pure sin.

"What kind?" I asked, half-laughing, the "new me" curious.

"Something special," he winked, unrolling it. I had no idea what it was, Vegas's poison. I laughed, faith screaming, don't do it! but dove in. Brad heated the foil, fumes rising like rocket fuel. We inhaled, and *boom*—I was on a spaceship, G-forces pinning me to the bed. "Can't sit up!" I slurred, giggling. Brad howled, slapping my legs—*whack!*—jolting me upright. We collapsed, laughing till tears streamed, the drug turning us into idiots. Loose, fearless, and completely disregarding our girlfriends back at home, we suited up, operation "score some babes" on.

Brad's white Lamborghini roared to Cosmopolitan's Pure nightclub, my high making Vegas a blur. I was Neil Armstrong, lunar-bound, Brad cackling beside me. We valet-parked, strutting like pimps, suits crisp. The bouncer, a brick wall, eyed us—high, sloppy—and blocked the door. "Not tonight," he growled. Brad cursed, storming off, but my drug-fueled ego crashed. From king to nobody, I felt old-money eyes judging, paranoia spiking. I ducked into a bathroom, heart racing, every door-slam a threat—*Slater? Feds?* Users stared, seeing a tweaked-out fool. No sanctuary.

Outside, I slumped on a red cushioned bar seat, higher than Zion's peaks. Four gorgeous women caught my eye, their laughter a taunt. A slick pickup artist—Rolex, tailored blazer—worked them, ignoring the prettiest, charming her friends. Slow-motion, I read it: he made her crave his nod, then whisked her away with a whispered line, hand in hers. *Balls like watermelons*, I thought, awed, my high turning his game into Shakespeare. Brad and I? Dead fish, flopping.

The drug faded, but Vegas never sleeps. We taxied to Planet Hollywood's Heart Bar, neon pulsing. Admitted, our energy surged. "AMFs!" Brad bellowed, ordering Adios Motherfuckers—blue booze rockets. We chugged two each, buzz reigniting, and hit the dance floor, *Feel So Close* shaking us. Girl-radar on, we grabbed partners—Brad's a 6'2" giantess, mine a 220-pound bruiser. Beer goggles turned them into models. We spun, lights strobing, feeling like gods. Club closing, we led them, slurring romance, to the casino's lounge, sinking into plush couches. Then, chaos—kissing, groping, a public mess. Onlookers gagged; I cringe now, we were pigs in suits.

Brad, ever the hound, pushed his giantess to our motel, whispering promises for 20 minutes. She and my girl vanished, poof, leaving us buzzed, frustrated, and alone. "Vegas, man," Brad laughed, slumping. We taxied to the Stratosphere, the smart call, avoiding a DUI rap. Day nine done, eight days left, six cars to steal. Cody's threats—"Slater's coming"—lurked, **Jaxons**'s betrayal and **Julie Broadwell**'s Fed tip tightening a net we couldn't see. My drug, booze, and lust scarred me, **Emma**'s smile a ghost. Greed—my chase, Cody's scam, Ethan's jaws—owned us, but tonight, we'd ruled Vegas, if only in our heads.

CHAPTER 12: HANGOVERS TO SUCCESS

Las Vegas was a vampire, draining souls under a desert sun.

Rihanna's We Found Love echoed from the Vegas Strip, a hymn for hopeless highs. I woke up at 3 p.m. in a Stratosphere motel, head pounding like a jackhammer. Six cars—my BMW, Camaro, Challenger, Range Rover and Brad's, Lamborghini, Bugatti—sat in our lot, half of our 12 Vegas Highline rides back, Last night's party, AMFs, and girls left me wrecked, Emma's smile a ghost. Brad groaned on the opposite queen size bed, his phone flashing with all the missed calls from Ashley, his desperate girlfriend. My phone buzzed—a text from Cody: "Blue BMW 550, southwest Vegas, auto shop. Don't fuck this up." His cooperation held, another car meant another win.

We stumbled up, showered off the booze stink, and shuffled through the Stratosphere casino, slots chiming like superficial winnings. Vegas started to feel like home, its grime cozy. Pulling out of the parking garage, I eyed the seedy hotel south, a den of evil—drugs, deals, worse. Left onto Vegas Blvd, right past panhandlers with hollow eyes, shifty types slinking by the World's Largest Gift Shop. Their glances screamed trouble—what were they hiding? Right again, past a tower complex, Treasures strip club winking, then onto the freeway. Vegas's dark side glared—evil in the open, my Mormon bubble pricked.

Cody's directions led to a southwest auto body shop, dust swirling. A blue BMW 550 gleamed out back, leather seats pristine, cologne heavy. The console held change, condoms—pimp's ride or drug runner's? High mileage screamed abuse, like every Highline car. Seven down, five to go. Brad fist-bumped me, grinning, "Another score, bro." Confidence surged, but **Jaxon**'s shadow loomed. Cody had tipped him off. Jaxon was in debt, drug-addled like Brad, but worse. Jaxon was married to **Lila** with a kid, chased drugs, girls, and power, his speed-dial harem and Cody's clout was feeding his vices. Jaxon had sister, a rehab wreck who'd lost her kids, mirrored his "rich family problems." Jaxon was coming to Vegas, to visit us, but really looking to pickup a score from Cody.

We hit Caesars Palace at 5 p.m., stomachs growling. Over steaks, Jaxon swaggered in. "Heard you're killing it," he said, eyes glassy—coke or worse. His Armani outfit screamed Brad's style, and I felt it creeping into me—cocky strut, vice's pull. After dinner we decided to buy some "yards"—three-foot icy cocktails, vodka burning. Shopping followed, Caesars' Armani store bleeding my last $1,500 on cloths, Brad and Jaxon egging me on. At northwest outlet malls, Jaxon's "Vegas rules" mantra pushed more buys, silver chains, Gucci shades. My Mormon core screamed, but I was theirs.

Night fell, Jaxon ditching us to party with Cody—drugs, no doubt. Brad and I, in new threads, hit the Stratosphere's lounge, glowing. Two Canadian girls—blonde, leggy, all giggles—lit our radar. "Mind if we join?" I asked, sliding up, Brad's grin backing me. They nodded, sipping cosmos. Names swapped—Chloe and Mia, here for "fun." Same page, baby. Drinks flowed—whiskey sours, then shots—our questions slurring: "Where ya from?" "Vegas vibe cool?"

Canada, good times, blah blah. Inhibitions melted, Chloe's hand on my thigh, Mia giggling at Brad's dumb jokes. Drunk, we had a plan: the Stratosphere's top, 1,149 feet up, Vegas sprawling like a lover.

Elevator up, the girls clung, lips brushing necks. At the observation deck, city lights dazzled, romantic as a drunk's poem. We made out, sloppy, urgent, Chloe's perfume drowning Emma's ghost. Twenty minutes in, Brad blurted, "Let's grab drinks in our room!" Brad's code for *it's time to fuck*, and we all knew it. Back to the motel, clothes hit the floor, a blur of skin and bad choices. No numbers swapped—Chloe and Mia, gone forever by dawn.

Five cars left, eight days to do it. Greed—my chase, hungover but alive, success tasting like sin.

CHAPTER 13: TWEEDLEDEE AND TWEEDLEDUM

L as Vegas was turning into a neon snake pit, its desert heat coiling around your soul. Skrillex's Bangarang thumped from a passing lowrider, 2012's pulse for reckless idiots. I was slowly gaining my cars back but in the process I was losing my soul. Only a few cars left to reclaim. Cody Vance's leads kept us rolling, his "Slater's coming" threats, a dull roar. But Jaxon was a virus—arrogant, coked-up, chasing his, his dad's, and his mistress's cars. His basketball-star swagger and manipulative bullshit—pitting me against Brad, bragging like a punk—had me ready to ditch him. The greed, Cody's con, Ethan Kassab's empire—was a noose, but I'd cut it, or choke trying.

Brad, was loyal but weak to Jaxon's vibe—drugs, bravado, chaos. We didn't trust Jaxon's loose lips, so we shuttled cars to St. George, hiding them with friends and family. Back in Vegas, leads dried up—two days, zero cars, just Jaxon's yap: "I'm the man, Dal." By day three, I'd had it. "Brad, take this clown and check the eastside complex," I snapped, heading to a west Vegas lot. My lead? A bust—empty pavement. As dusk fell, Brad called, voice a stoned giggle.

"You're not gonna believe this!" he slurred.

"What?" I growled, patience thin.

"Jaxon—uh,—and I hit the gated complex. Found my other Mercedes, Jaxons's Audi, your CL550!"

"You get 'em?" I asked, hope spiking.

"Well…" Brad laughed, high as a kite. "We got two, not yours. Sorry, D. Listen—hot hooker out front, guarding the cars. We said they're stolen, threatened cops. She stonewalled, then her pimp—big Black dude, all swagger—rolls out with more girls, sexy as hell. Arguing, yelling, no dice. I calmed it, offered weed. We got blazed, and they chilled, gave us the Audi and my Mercedes!"

"You're high *now*?" I roared, picturing my CL550 slipping away.

"High off my ass!" Brad cackled. I was livid—me, I'd have chained myself to that car. He sensed it. "Sorry, Dal, I fucked up." Then Jaxon's voice, snatching the phone: "Yo, Dal, chill! I got the pimp's number. He's cool, wants to help. Your girl's 'working' tonight—CL550's hers. I get shit done, right? Back by 10:30."

"Fine," I spat, hanging up. Tweedledee and Tweedledum—Brad and Jaxon, stoned, partying with pimps while my $120K car sat in a hooker's hands. Nine cars down, three to go, but this was a circus. Jaxon's "pimp pal" story smelled like coke-fueled bullshit, but I prayed it held. Inside the complex, I imagined it: Brad sparking a joint, Jaxon flirting, girls giggling, pimp nodding, cars forgotten. My blood boiled—greed made me hustle, but these clowns chased highs.

Vegas's neon hid the real war. Cody's leads came steady, but something was brewing with **Slater and his Dad**, the Feds circling via **Julie Broadwell**'s tip (day one). Jaxon's betrayal—drugs, girls, Cody's orbit—stank worse, his mistress **Julie was** able to snitch. Brad's weed stunt echoed Chapter 11's drug haze, my own alcohol abuse, girl-chasing sins (Chapter 12) not far off. St. George runs kept us safe, but **Emma**'s fading smile burned. Three cars, ~six days left. Greed—my fight, vegas ruled us. I gripped my Glock for a sense of security, fury my fuel, vowing to finish this, Tweedledee and Tweedledum be damned.

CHAPTER 14 RUN-IN WITH THE DEVIL

L as Vegas began to feel like a neon graveyard, its desert dusk bleeding red. Deadmau5's Ghosts 'n' Stuff hummed from a distant club, dirge for broken dreams. But the house of cards built by—Slater Kassab Ethan Kassab, Jaxon—was begining to crumble, Julie Broadwell's Fed tip sparking whispers of a Utah probe. A text from Cody hit: "Brad's BMW, impound lot, east Vegas. Dusk. Be there." Our first face-to-face with Cody since the contracts, the devil himself.

Brad, cursed, "That bastard better deliver." We rolled to the lot, chain-link and razor wire glinting under a blood-orange sky. Cody pulled up in a Mercedes SLS AMG, $200K of criminal swagger, its gullwing doors mocking us. He stepped out, 24, Mormon-raised gone rogue—5'11", 210 pounds, blond fohawk, blue eyes piercing like ice, sharp nose, square chin. His cool, calm stride screamed control, no smile, no warmth, just business to save his ass. Brad and I were his problem, and he knew it.

"You got our car?" I asked, voice steel, sizing him up.

"Inside," Cody said, flat, leading us through the gate. No small talk, no games—Slater's heat had him spooked. The navy blue BMW 535i sat battered, front window smashed, interior looted. "Son of a bitch!" Brad roared, kicking a tire. "Brand new, needs four grand to fix!" Cody shrugged, tossing a $250 check to the lot clerk, then peeled out, Mercedes roaring, gone like smoke. Ten cars down, two to go, but Brad's rage burned—greed's price, etched in glass.

We had ten cars in Vegas, a ticking bomb. Plan: drive two to St. George, recruit Ashley, Brad's girlfriend, and his parents to ferry the rest. Each ride—my five, Brad's five—hit Utah's red rocks, hidden with cousins and friends. Brad's endgame? Unclear, maybe flip 'em. Mine? Blackmail. I'd scoured Valorre Auto's contracts, finding gold: loan fraud, my name forged across multiple pages. Vince Cole, the broker, was either Cody's pawn or Ethan's dog— didn't matter. I marched into his St. George office, papers in hand, Glock in my jacket.

"Vince," I said, slamming the contracts down, "you're buying my cars back, full price—$480K—or I turn you in for fraud and sue you to hell." His eyes, wide with fear, screamed *screwed*. Cody, Slater, Ethan—he knew the net was tightening. "Okay," he croaked, "I'll clean 'em, sell 'em." Victim or crook? His sweat didn't lie—he was in deep, and I had him. Control felt sweet, greed my blade.

But the scam was imploding. I'd stopped payments, bill collectors hounding me daily. I dodged, lied, stalling for Vince's sales to dodge bankruptcy. Cody vanished post-impound, ignoring texts, calls. **Greg**, Jaxon's dad, and other suckers—dealers, renters—panicked, payments gone. Jaxon got burned too, his drug-fueled loyalty to Cody worthless. Rumors flew: Cody dead? Hiding with millions? One truth cut through—Julie's Fed tip had sparked a storm. Bob Hodges, a Fed investigator, called me, voice calm but probing. My gut twisted—after a St. George cop threatened jail when I sought help, I trusted no badge. Still, Utah and Feds were moving, eyeing Cody, Slater, Ethan, Jaxon, and sadly us the vicitms.

Banks chased owners, even those paying, demanding cars' locations. The CL550 and Brad's Porsche Cayman? Vanished, ghosts in Vegas's haze. Ten of 12 cars, a bitter win. Financial ruin spread— dealers, renters, us—greed's collateral damage. **Emma**'s fading smile haunted me, my Mormon soul scarred by alcohol, drugs, girls. Slater's bat, Ethan's shadow, Feds' net—time was short. Two cars left. I gripped my Glock, control slipping, the devil's laugh echoing in Cody's taillights.

CHAPTER 15 THE LAST STAND

S t. George, May 2012, was a red-rock prison, its nights heavy
with defeat. Swedish House Mafia's Don't You Worry Child Drifted
from a neighbor's radio, 2012's lament for lost fights. I was missing
one: my CL550. Brad his Porsche Cayman was gone. Ten of 12 cars,
a hollow score. Cody Vance's disappearance left us dangling, Slater
Kassab and Ethan Kassab's empire cracking under a Fed probe
sparked by Julie Broadwell's tip. Now, Slater's gangsters prowled,
hitting registered addresses—Vegas lots, St. George homes—
hunting our cars.

Two weeks since **Jaxon Reed**'s pimp promise (week two), the guy
ghosted, his number dead. Brad quit, gave up, his fifth car lost.
"Kentucky, man," he said, packing for alarm sales. "Good money,
fresh start." He and Jaxon, were buddies again, trading shit-talk but
recruiting each other for summer hustles. Jaxon's drugged-up grin at
Brad's invite—"Vegas sucked, let's roll"—left me cold. They bailed
for Kentucky, leaving me in St. George, alone, my CL550 a ghost.
Brad's parents, saints, gave me their guest room, a month's grace.
Emma's fading smile burned, my Mormon soul drowning in guilt
and pain.

I hunted. Brad's last CL550 sighting—Vegas gated complex, that hooker's den—became my obsession. I drove my Range Rover, parked a block away, and camped two days, living on Red Bull, Glock ready. Day two, 5 a.m., desert chill biting, I saw it—my CL550, gleaming under a streetlamp, key in my pocket. Adrenaline roared, heart a war drum. The girl—same one from Jaxon's fiasco—slid out, heels clicking, and entered her apartment. I waited, breath shallow, then crept, scaling the fence, silent as sin. Halfway over, her door swung—she bolted to the car, engine snarling, and sped off. I froze, wire cutting my palms, watching taillights fade. Last chance, gone.

Back in St. George, banks hounded, calls relentless. Vince Cole, flopped—no car sales, his fear useless. Sick of dodging the banks, I snapped, "They're at Valorre Auto, take 'em!" One by one, banks repoed my five rides, each tow-truck clank a nail in my coffin. Brad, in Kentucky, faced the same—his cars, gone. We hired a lawyer, a grizzled St. George vet. "Cody's vanished, Valorre's a shell," he said. "Chapter 7 bankruptcy, boys—only way." Filing felt like death—half a million, wiped, but scars stayed. My CL550, Brad's Porsche Cayman? Never surfaced—no registries, no records, ghosts of greed.

Slater's thugs kept coming, tires screeching at night, shadows at Brad's parents' place. Bob Hodges, the Fed investigator, called again, voice sharp: "Talk, Dallin, or you're next." I stonewalled, St. George's crooked cop still souring me. Jaxon's betrayal—Julie's tip, his drugged-up loyalty to Cody—fueled the Feds, targeting Ethan, Slater, Cody and all the victims. Banks crushed owners, even payers, repossessing blindly. **Greg**, Jaxons's dad, lost millions, others ruined. Greed's fallout buried us all. Summer loomed, Kentucky calling, but my fight died in that 5 a.m. dust, **American greed** my judge, jury, executioner.

CHAPTER 16: NO
WINNERS

St. George, 2013, was a desert scar, its silence louder than
Vegas's neon. Imagine Dragons' Radioactive blared from a passing
truck, anthem for shattered worlds. I was Dallin Barnes, 26, a
Mormon kid, my $480K car loans erased by Chapter 7 bankruptcy,
but the weight lingered. Brad Covington, $600K wiped, stood beside
me, both of us with 10 of 12 Vegas Highline cars—my Mercedes,
Camaro, Challenger, BMW 550, BMW 750Li; his Range Rover,
Lamborghini, Bugatti, two Mercedes—repoed or lost. My CL550,
his Porsche Cayman, ghosts forever. Cody Vance's scam, Slater
Kassab's threats, Ethan Kassab's empire—it all crashed, Julie
Broadwell's Fed tip (2011) igniting a firestorm. The Feds raided
Ethan's world, cuffs snapping on Cody, Slater, Vince Cole, and
Mitch Carver, but Ethan, the untouchable king, slipped free.
American greed—my hustle, Cody's con, Ethan's shadow—left no
winners, only survivors.

Utah's courts came hard, 2012's summer a blur of subpoenas. They
didn't just chase Cody and Slater; they slapped us all—me, Brad,
Jaxon, Greg, Julie, every buyer, every leaser—with equity
skimming charges and communications fraud for renting cars

through **Vegas Highline**. Media swarmed, newsstands screaming: *Victims or Crooks? Utah's Car Scam Scandal*. Reporters called us pawns, not perps, but plea deals stung: guilty, records sealed, clean in seven years—2019. Cody, caught in Vegas, cut a deal, his silver tongue spilling names for bigger fish, his multi-state crimes (Utah, Nevada, Arizona, California) handing the case to Feds. **Bob Hodges**, the Fed investigator, led the charge, dismantling Ethan's web, but the boss walked, a ghost in tailored suits.

I broke in 2011, **Emma**'s eyes—pure, trusting—haunting me. The alcohol, drugs, girls (2012) were sins I couldn't carry. "I'm not him anymore," I told her, voice cracking, ending us. Guilt won, but it freed me. I quit drugs, cold, my Mormon roots clawing back. Kentucky's summer, selling alarms with Brad and Jaxon, was my reset. We crushed it, door-to-door kings, commissions piling. By 2013, I'd made peace with my family, their prayers my anchor. I met her—my dream woman, all heart, no judgment—married her, a new dawn. St. George became home, my Glock 17 shelved, greed's scars fading.

Brad turned it around, too. Counseling healed him and Ashley, her forgiveness a miracle. Engaged, they stayed in St. George, Brad hunting deer, fishing rivers, sober and solid. But Jaxon, was a trainwreck. Kentucky's summer, he shone—top first-year rep, nearly winning a car, his basketball-star charm unstoppable. Then, darkness: beating **Lila**, cheating, drugs swallowing him. Suicidal, he got jumped by gangsters, his coke stash stolen. In revenge, he rammed a rival's car, high, raging. Cops found cocaine, charged him—assault with a deadly weapon, six counts of equity skimming, one communications fraud, felonies stacking. He broke his plea deal, partying over probation, and prison loomed, his dad's millions paying his debts, not his sins.

The scam's fallout was brutal. **Greg**, Utah's insurance ace, sued Cody and Valorre **Auto**, outcome, winner but nothing to collect, lost in court fog. **Slater** and Cody shut **Vegas Highline**, charged, now FBI prey, prison for years. **Vince Cole**, a greasy broker, got arrested, bailed out, but Valorre **Auto** died, bought, rebranded. The Kassab's Aurum **Cars** closed, dodging headlines. **Mitch Carver**, the finance guy, fled to Missouri, subpoenas chasing. Victims—dealers, renters, dreamers—bled millions, lives wrecked. **Jaxon's dad** paid his and Jaxon's debts, but most drowned.

The lesson? Trust is a trap. If it gleams too bright—like Cody's Mercedes, Ethan's empire—it's a lie. **American greed** burned us, from my $480K hustle to Jaxon's drugged-up fall. News articles, searchable online—*St George's Auto Fraud Case Utah Car Scam Bust, 2012*—tell the tale, but scars speak louder. I'm clean, married, whole, but no one won. Greed's game leaves only ashes.

EPILOGUE

Utah, 2025. The mountain wind carries a quiet I've grown to love, a far cry from the neon scream of Vegas during those hellish years. I'm Dallin Barnes, now 40, a husband, a father of four, my days of chasing stolen cars and dodging criminals long buried. The Vegas Highline scam—those three weeks of heists, betrayals, and bankruptcy—left scars, but they shaped me. My wife's laughter, my kids' footsteps, my steady career—they're my redemption, proof I clawed back from greed's edge. My friend, still in St. George, hunting with his wife and kids, their marriage strong. The fate of some of the others in this book still haunt me—prison swallowed them, for their crimes their drug-fueled spirals a warning etched in my bones. Cody Vance, Slater Bryce, and the others faded into headlines, their empire dust. Ethan Bryce, untouchable, vanished, a ghost of ambition. The lesson lingers: trust is fragile, greed a thief. I walk forward, faith renewed, carrying the weight of 2011-2012 not as shame, but as strength.

AFTERWORD

Looking back on the neon haze of 2011-2013, I'm struck by how a single choice—chasing the gleam of quick riches—pulled me into the abyss of the Vegas Highline scam. Writing this book, I relived the thrill of reclaiming cars, the chaos of Vegas nights, and the sting of betrayal from those I trusted. I'm embarrassed by some of my decisions—signing those contracts, diving into drugs and debauchery, letting greed cloud my Mormon roots. Those choices cost me relationships, my peace, and nearly my future. But from that wreckage, I grew tougher, found love, and rebuilt with my family. This story isn't just mine; it's a mirror for anyone tempted by promises too bright to be true. To you, the reader, thank you for walking this desert road with me. Your time with these pages means more than I can say—it's proof that even in our darkest stumbles, there's a story worth telling, a lesson worth learning.

BOOKS BY THIS AUTHOR

Dollars & Sense: Empowering You With Financial Literacy

💰 Teach Your Family the Money Skills They Need for a Lifetime of Success! 💰

In today's fast-paced world, financial education is more important than ever—and it's never too early to start! Dollars and Sense: Empowering You with Financial Literacy is a fun, engaging, and easy-to-understand guide that teaches families the essential knowledge they need to make smart money choices.

From understanding the basics of money, earning, saving, and spending to more advanced concepts like investing, budgeting, and even starting a small business, this book turns financial literacy into an exciting adventure. With relatable stories, real-life examples, and interactive activities, families will gain the confidence to manage money wisely and build habits that set them up for future success.

📖 Inside This Book, You Will Learn:
✓ What money is and how it works
✓ The importance of saving and setting financial goals
✓ How to make smart spending decisions
✓ The basics of budgeting in a fun and easy way
✓ How to start earning money at any age
✓ The power of investing and how money can grow over time
✓ How to avoid common money mistakes and develop healthy financial habits

Perfect for families with children ages 10-18, Dollars and Sense is an essential resource for parents, teachers, and caregivers who want to give kids a head start on financial independence. Whether your child dreams of becoming a young entrepreneur, saving for something special, or just making better financial choices, this book is the perfect roadmap to financial success!

Give your child the gift of financial knowledge—because smart money habits start young!

Recruit, Lead, Succeed: Success Through Influence

Success isn't just about what you achieve-it's about who you bring along for the journey. Recruit, Lead, Succeed: Success Through Influence by Dallin Barnes is a powerful guide for those looking to build high-performing teams, lead with impact, and create lasting success through the art of influence.

In this book, Dallin shares the key strategies behind effective recruiting and leadership, showing how the ability to attract and develop the right people is the foundation of long-term financial and professional success. Whether you're in sales, business, or leadership, this book will equip you with the skills to inspire, motivate, and lead others to greatness.

Inside, you'll learn:

The fundamental principles of top recruiters and influential leaders.
How to identify, attract, and retain top talent.
The role of resilience, adaptability, and persistence in leadership.
Strategies to create a winning culture and drive long-term success.
How influence-not just authority-drives real leadership.
Through real-world examples, actionable insights, and a proven framework, Recruit, Lead, Succeed reveals how leadership and recruitment are the cornerstones of financial and career success. By mastering these skills, you'll not only achieve your own goals but also help others rise-creating a lasting impact in business and

beyond.

If you're ready to elevate your leadership, strengthen your influence, and build a legacy of success, this book is your roadmap to making it happen.

Obsolete: What to Do Before AI Replaces Your Job

Obsolete: What to Do Before AI Replaces Your Job

Book Summary:

Obsolete is a survival guide for one of the most urgent shifts in human history—the rise of artificial intelligence and the end of work as we know it. As machines grow smarter, faster, and more capable than ever before, millions of jobs across every industry are vanishing. But this isn't a doomsday prophecy. It's a wake-up call—and a blueprint.

This book reveals how to future-proof your income, mindset, and identity in a world where AI threatens to replace not just labor, but logic, creativity, and decision-making. From the death of traditional careers to the explosion of micro-entrepreneurship, Obsolete explores how technology is rewriting the rules of business, education, healthcare, creativity, and personal fulfillment.

You'll learn:

Why even "safe" white- and blue-collar jobs are at risk
Which human skills are truly irreplaceable—and how to master them
How to pivot, reskill, and reinvent your career midstream
Where to invest your time, money, and energy as industries evolve
What to teach your children to prepare them for a future without job security
How to build real human connection and purpose in a machine-run world
Backed by real-world trends and a practical 5-year action plan, Obsolete isn't just about surviving the AI age—it's about rising

through it with clarity, confidence, and control.

You are not powerless. You are not replaceable. But you must act—before the world decides for you.

www.ingramcontent.com/pod-product-compliance
Lightning Source LLC
Chambersburg PA
CBHW070249290326
41930CB00042B/2989